W5/12 W4/15 W3/48 W3/22

Dutch Colonies in America

by Mary Englar

Content Adviser: Richard J. Bell, Ph.D.,
Assistant Professor, Department of History,
University of Maryland

Reading Adviser: Alexa L. Sandmann, Ed.D.,
Professor of Literacy, College and Graduate School of Education,
Kent State University

Compass Point Books ✦ Minneapolis, Minnesota

Compass Point Books
151 Good Counsel Drive
P.O. Box 669
Mankato, MN 56002-0669

This book was manufactured with paper containing
at least 10 percent post-consumer waste.

On the cover: Governor Peter Stuyvesant and Dutch settlers meet with Indians in 1660 New Amsterdam;
wood engraving, 1855

Photographs ©: The Granger Collection, New York, cover, 11, 16, 20, 21, 25, 26, 29, 30, 38; Prints Old
and Rare, back cover (far left); Library of Congress, back cover, 39, 41; MPI/Getty Images, 5; Bettmann/
Corbis, 6, 7; North Wind Picture Archives, 8, 10, 14, 17, 19, 22, 23, 24, 27, 31, 34, 35, 36; Library of
Congress/Map Division, 13; Stock Montage/Getty Images, 33; Private Collection/Philip Mould Ltd,
London/The Bridgeman Art Library, 40.

Editor: Jennifer VanVoorst
Page Production: Bobbie Nuytten
Photo Researcher: Svetlana Zhurkin
Cartographer: XNR Productions, Inc.
Library Consultant: Kathleen Baxter

Art Director: LuAnn Ascheman-Adams
Creative Director: Keith Griffin
Editorial Director: Nick Healy
Managing Editor: Catherine Neitge

Library of Congress Cataloging-in-Publication Data
Englar, Mary.
  Dutch colonies in America / by Mary Englar.
    p. cm. — (We the people)
  Includes index.
  ISBN 978-0-7565-3837-8 (library binding)
1. New Netherland—History—Juvenile literature. 2. New York (State)—History—Colonial period,
ca. 1600–1775—Juvenile literature. 3. Dutch—North America—History—Juvenile literature.
4. Netherlands—Colonies—America—Juvenile literature. 5. Frontier and pioneer life—New
Netherland—Juvenile literature. 6. Frontier and pioneer life—New York (State)—Juvenile literature.
7. North America—History—Colonial period, ca. 1600–1775—Juvenile literature. I. Title. II. Series.
  F122.1.E54 2009
  974.7'302—dc22   2008007211

Visit Compass Point Books on the Internet at *www.compasspointbooks.com*
or e-mail your request to *custserv@compasspointbooks.com*

TABLE OF CONTENTS

A "VERY GOOD LAND"

On a misty September morning in 1609, Captain Henry Hudson and his crew readied their ship, the *Half Moon,* to enter a large bay on North America's east coast. The 85-foot (26-meter) *Half Moon* rose and dipped in the rough water at the mouth of the bay. Then, with a good wind behind it, the *Half Moon* headed north across the bay.

As the fog burned off, the men saw a beautiful, green landscape. Hills covered with trees 60 feet (18 m) tall rose from the water's edge. Shorebirds fished in the marshes near the coast. Schools of fish swam alongside the ship. Hudson's shipmate wrote that the area was "very good land to fall in with, and a pleasant land to see."

The next day, American Indians came out to the *Half Moon* in canoes. The Indians wore deerskin clothing and copper necklaces. They greeted the sailors and offered them gifts. In return, Hudson offered them knives and glass beads. Over the next several days, the Indians brought dried fruit, corn bread, oysters, and fur pelts.

Hudson explored the land around the bay. He was looking for the Northwest Passage to Asia. Hudson hoped he had found this passage in the deep, wide river on the north side of the bay. For several weeks, he sailed up the river that came to be known as the Hudson River.

Henry Hudson and his crew sailed up what is known today as the Hudson River to present-day Albany, New York.

A 20th-century painting by Jean Leon Gerome Ferris of Hudson's encounter with local Indians

About 160 miles (256 kilometers) north of the bay, the river became too shallow for ships.

Although he had not discovered the Northwest Passage, Hudson had found a land rich in resources. He returned to the Netherlands and reported to the Dutch East India Company merchants who had hired him. The

Hudson traded with Native Americans for furs, which he brought back to Europe.

merchants saw the heavy fur pelts he brought back and listened to his stories of huge forests. Furs and timber were valuable trade goods in Europe. The Dutch East India Company soon claimed the land along the Hudson River for the Netherlands.

NEW NETHERLAND

The land that Hudson had explored became New Netherland and included the area along the Hudson, the Connecticut, and the Delaware rivers. The Dutch East India Company did not plan to settle this land. It wanted to build fur-trading posts.

The Dutch East India Company had its warehouses and shipyard in Amsterdam, the Netherlands.

In the early 1600s, North America was mostly unknown to Europeans. Sailors had fished and traded along North America's Atlantic coast for many years, but they did not stay. The American Indians who traded fur pelts with the European sailors were curious and fearful. They wanted the metal cooking pots and tools the sailors had. But they also knew that some European sailors captured Indians and sold them into slavery in Europe.

The Indians near the Hudson River belonged to many different nations. The Delaware, or the Lenape, lived along the Delaware River and the southern part of the Hudson River. They had traded with Europeans before, and they were cautious in their trade with Hudson. At times, they attacked his ship. Once, one of his men was killed, and two others were hurt.

At the north end of the Hudson River, the Mahicans lived by the water. To the west, along the Mohawk River, lived the Five Nations of the Iroquois. The Mahicans and Iroquois did not speak the same language. They were

Native Americans of the area lived in longhouses.

often at war with each other over hunting, fishing, and
trading rights.

The Dutch traders found the Mahicans friendly and
willing to trade. They shared some land along the river in
exchange for gifts. In 1614, the Dutch built a trading post
on the Hudson River and named it Fort Nassau. It was

10

Dutch traders had a friendly business relationship with many Indian tribes.

later rebuilt as Fort Orange. Dutch traders came every summer to trade tools, glass beads, and wool cloth for fur pelts.

The pelts sold well in Europe and made the Dutch traders wealthy. In 1621, a group of Dutch merchants asked the government of the Netherlands to give them a charter to protect the New Netherland trade. The government charter gave these merchants a monopoly on all trade to and from the lands that bordered the Atlantic Ocean. When the charter was granted later that year, the merchants formed the Dutch West India Company.

The colony of New Netherland included parts of what are now the states of New York, New Jersey, Connecticut, and Delaware. In exchange for the charter, the West India Company promised to send settlers to claim the land for the Netherlands. In January 1624, the first ship sailed for New Netherland with 30 families aboard. The West India Company promised settlers their own land if they worked six years for the company.

The Dutch knew that the rivers would be the highways in this new land. The company divided the families into three groups and sent them to build settlements along New Netherland's major rivers. Some families were sent to Fort Orange on the Hudson River,

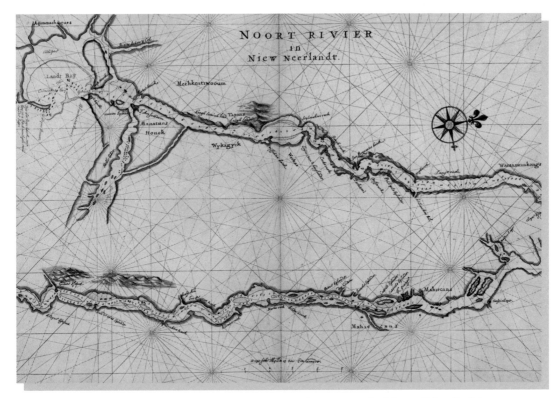

NOORT RIVIER
in
Niew Neerlandt.

A 17th-century map of the Hudson River, known at the time as the Noort (North) River

others to the Delaware River, and the last settled along the
Connecticut River. Each group had fewer than 50 people.

The settlers began clearing trees so they could plant
crops. At first, the Fort Orange families dug pits in the
ground for their homes. They lined the walls with wood
and made roofs from bark. Life was difficult, but the
settlers found plenty to eat. Large herds of deer lived in

13

Dutch settlers welcomed new arrivals to New Netherland.

the forests. Fish, oysters, lobsters, and clams were delicious and easy to catch. One settler wrote that if they had cows and pigs, "we would not wish to return to Holland, for whatever we desire in the paradise of Holland, is here to be found."

14

NEW AMSTERDAM

The first settlers in what is today known as New York Bay chose Nut Island, present-day Governor's Island, for their town. It was small but easy to protect. As more settlers and farm animals arrived from the Netherlands, the settlers began grazing their cattle on a larger island a short distance away from Nut Island. The Indians called the larger island Manna-hata, which meant "land of many hills." The colonists called it Manhattan Island.

The first year went well for the colonists. The West India Company set rules for what the colonists could do. The Indians came to trade beaver and otter pelts and were happy to receive pots, glassware, needles, and knives in exchange. The company told the colonists to trade fairly with the Indians and to make sure that "no one [does] the Indians any harm or violence." The colonists knew they were greatly outnumbered by the Indians. Most followed the rules and kept the peace.

The Dutch West India Company made sure colonists traded fairly with Indians.

The company also warned the Dutch commander of Fort Orange not to take sides in conflicts between the Indian nations. But the commander formed an alliance with the Mahicans. In 1626, a band of Mahicans asked the commander to help them fight off a group of Iroquois. The Iroquois also wanted to trade with the Dutch, and the Mahicans did not want the competition. The commander

16

agreed to help the Mahicans.

Only a few miles from Fort Orange, a band of Iroquois attacked the rival group. The Iroquois killed nearly all of the Mahicans and four of the Dutch. The commander was killed in the fighting. When the colonists at the fort heard about the attack, they fled by ship downriver to Nut Island. The colonists met to decide what to do. They voted for a new commander from their group. Peter Minuit, a businessman, was elected.

An Iroquois warrior

Minuit sent messengers to bring the colonists who lived along the Delaware and the Connecticut rivers to New York Bay for their safety. Minuit knew that Nut Island was too small to support a large settlement. He saw that Manhattan Island had good flat land for farming. If the colonists built a fort

17

at the southern tip of the island, they could defend the settlement from Indian attacks.

Small bands of Lenape Indians lived on Manhattan

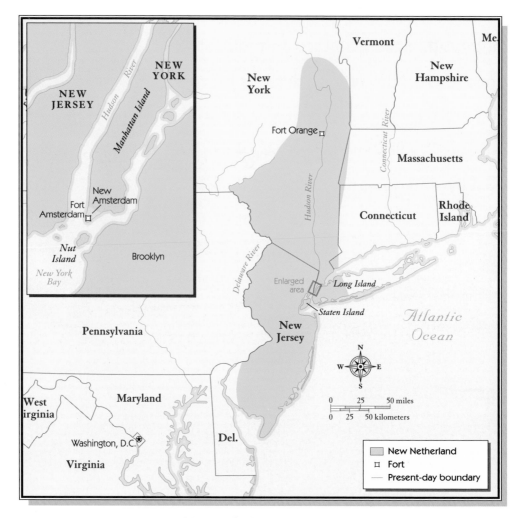

New Netherland occupied parts of present-day New York, New Jersey, Connecticut, and Delaware.

Island. Minuit met with the chiefs and offered to trade for some land for his settlement. He gave the Indians goods worth 60 Dutch guilders. The Indians of Manhattan did not use money, but exactly what goods Minuit gave them is unknown.

In 1626, 200 colonists from all parts of New Netherland settled on Manhattan Island. Minuit named the

Peter Minuit traded goods with local Indians in exchange for Manhattan Island.

VRYHEDEN

By de Vergaderinghe van de Negenthiene vande Geoctroyeerde West-Indische Compagnie vergunt aen allen den ghenen / die eenighe Colonien in Nieu-Nederlandt sullen planten.

In het licht ghegheven

Om bekent te maken wat Profijten ende Voordeelen aldaer in Nieu-Nederlandt, voor de Coloniers ende der selver Patroonen ende Meesters, midtsgaders de Participanten, die de Colonien aldaer planten, zijn becomen,

Westindjen Kan sijn Nederlands grovt gewin Verkleynt sonjands Macht brengt silver platen in.

T'AMSTELREDAM,

By Marten Iansz Brandt Boeckvercooper / woonende by de nieuwe Kerck/in de Gereformeerde Catechismus, Anno 1630.

A 1630 charter by the West India Company reserved the island of Manhattan for the use of the company.

new settlement New Amsterdam, after the largest city in the Netherlands. Minuit purchased Staten Island four years later for "Duffels, Kittles, Axes, Hoes, Wampum" and other small trade goods.

The Lenape agreed to share Manhattan Island with the Dutch in exchange for trade goods. They also expected the Dutch to protect them from their enemies. The Indians continued to live on Manhattan Island until at least 1675.

BUILDING A NEW COLONY

New Netherland colonists were quite diverse. The colonists came from the Netherlands, but they were not all Dutch. In the 1600s, the Netherlands was home to many immigrants from around Europe. Belgians, Germans, French, Scandinavians, and English came to the Netherlands. Most came for religious freedom. The Dutch were tolerant of cultural differences and did not enforce a national religion.

These immigrant groups saw opportunity in North America. Married couples and young families came to New Netherland to work for the West

Dutch settlers strolled along a canal in New Amsterdam.

21

India Company. They built a fort, a storehouse, a windmill, and new houses. Farmers grew crops to supply the soldiers stationed at the colony's forts. Many also traded for pelts that they sold to the company for a small profit.

New Netherland was different from other North American colonies. English people had settled most of the early colonies. These colonists spoke the same language. In New Amsterdam, however, one traveler reported that

Colonists played a game called "bowls" in New Netherland.

more than 18 languages were spoken in different parts of the colony. The diverse colonists brought their languages, religions, and cultures to New Netherland.

The West India Company named a director-general to oversee shipping and trade. The director-general made the laws, but he did not have enough soldiers to enforce them. As the colony grew, so did its problems. New Amsterdam's good harbor attracted pirates and smugglers. The streets were filled with drunken men fighting after the taverns closed. The mix of families, traders, soldiers, and sailors made New Amsterdam a lively but dangerous town.

A street preacher spoke to the crowd in New Amsterdam.

KIEFT'S WAR

While the New Netherland colonists struggled to build their towns, the West India Company continued to lose money. Thousands of pelts and shiploads of timber were sent to the Netherlands every year, but the colony did not pay for itself. The company had to pay soldiers to protect the colonists and Indian allies. The company decided that a tougher director-general was needed. In 1638, the company chose William Kieft to lead New Netherland.

The Dutch West India Company warehouse stored goods to be shipped back to the Netherlands.

Kieft was instructed to solve the problems of the colony and find a way to increase company profits.

When Kieft arrived in New Amsterdam, he looked for ways to cut the

24

amount of money the company paid for pelts and lumber. From the earliest days, New Netherland colonists used trade goods and beads to buy Indian pelts. They soon discovered that the Indians accepted strings of polished shells called wampum. The best wampum came from skilled beadmakers on Long Island. Kieft learned that many colonists accepted dirty, unpolished wampum in trade. He ordered that only the best, polished wampum would be accepted for trade. This raised the price for many trade goods, supplies, and services.

The company supplied soldiers at three forts in New Netherland. The soldiers protected colonists and, according to land agreements, promised to protect the Indians who lived on the

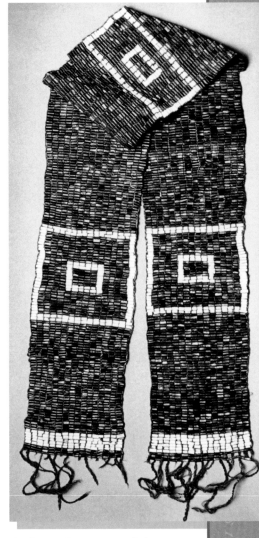

An Iroquois wampum belt

25

land. To raise money to pay for the soldiers, Kieft ordered the Indians to pay a tax of pelts, corn, or wampum.

The colonists knew this was a bad idea. They had signed land agreements that allowed the local Indians use of the land and protection against enemies. Kieft ordered the tax anyway. Most chiefs ignored the tax, but Kieft was

A 19th-century engraving of Dutch colonists and Indians trading at New Amsterdam

determined to make the Indians pay. About this time, a farm lost several hogs to thieves. Kieft did not investigate the crime. Instead, he sent soldiers to an Indian village. The soldiers killed several men there.

Kieft's forces marched on an Indian village in present-day Connecticut.

27

The Indians then attacked a Dutch farm and killed four men. Kieft wanted to punish the Indians. Again the colonists asked him not to start a war. The colonists had lived and traded with the Indians for many years. They knew they could not trap the animals that the Indians brought to them in such great numbers. Kieft did not see the Indians the same way. He wanted them to be afraid of the soldiers.

Kieft ordered his soldiers to attack Indian villages and burn them to the ground. Over several years, the soldiers attacked, and the Indians fought back. In 1643, Kieft ordered two groups of soldiers to destroy a Lenape village on Manhattan Island and another across the Hudson River. The soldiers attacked at night and killed 80 Indian men, women, and children.

The Indians were shocked to find that it was Dutch soldiers who had attacked them. Several bands of Lenape formed an alliance to fight back. The Indians attacked at night and burned farmhouses and crops. They killed

Kieft's forces attacked and killed 80 Indians in present-day Hoboken, New Jersey.

animals and kidnapped women and children. They attacked farms on Manhattan Island and burned down small towns on Long Island. The colonists fled to Fort Amsterdam for safety. For more than two years, the frightened colonists lived inside the fort.

A group of colonists wrote to the West India Company in Amsterdam. They told the company about

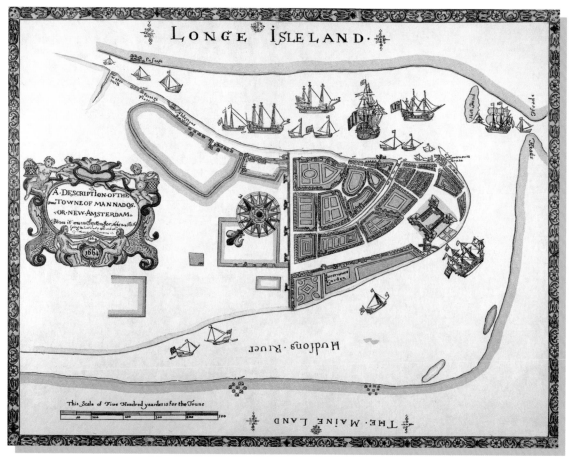

A 17th-century map of Manhattan Island and nearby Long Island

Kieft's war with the Indians. The colony was in terrible
shape, and Kieft did not listen to their advice. They asked
for a voice in governing the colony. The company owners
read the letters and agreed that Kieft must go. After all, he
had not made money for the company.

The company ordered Kieft to make peace with the Indians. In August 1645, Kieft and several Lenape chiefs signed a peace treaty. They agreed that future conflicts would be settled by discussion, not violence. The company also looked for a new leader for New Netherland. Unfortunately for the colonists, the company believed it needed an even stronger leader to enforce company rules.

The Dutch signed a peace treaty with the Indians in 1645.

A Tough New Director-General

In the spring of 1647, Director-General Peter Stuyvesant arrived in New York Harbor. He came with four ships of soldiers. Stuyvesant had worked for the West India Company for many years. The company owners were impressed with his skills. They promoted him to posts in Brazil, the Caribbean, and New Netherland. They believed he could manage the unruly colonists and finally make money for the company.

The colonists gathered on the waterfront to meet the new director. Stuyvesant wore military armor, and a sword hung at his side. When he stepped into a boat to come ashore, the colonists saw that he limped. Stuyvesant had lost part of his leg in a battle with Spanish soldiers over the Caribbean island of St. Martin. He wore a wooden leg decorated with silver. Stuyvesant promised the colonists that he would bring order and justice to New Netherland.

Stuyvesant wasted little time in enacting new laws. He saw that the fort's walls were crumbling and soldiers were camping in the courtyard. The fort needed to be rebuilt. The colonists threw their garbage in the streets and did not fence in their animals. He ordered them to fence their animals and said he would shoot loose pigs or cattle.

Peter Stuyvesant

Street fights happened frequently when taverns were open. Stuyvesant ordered taverns to close earlier and ordered that alcohol not be served on Sundays. If anyone used a knife in a fight, Stuyvesant sentenced him to six months in prison. He forced sailors to return to their ships at night.

Peter Stuyvesant managed all Dutch possessions in North America and the Caribbean.

Stuyvesant was tough, and he believed he was right. To make improvements, he passed a tax on wine and alcohol. The tax money was used to remove garbage, pave the streets, and rebuild the fort. He bought buckets to help put out fires. Night watchmen patrolled the streets after the taverns closed. Though Stuyvesant's many changes created

Stuyvesant's efforts made New Amsterdam a cleaner, safer place.

order in New Amsterdam, the colonists resented the loss of their freedom.

However, colonists finally got a say in local government. Some colonists had worked for years for their right to have a voice in colony decisions. The government in the Netherlands decided to give them the right to form a local government. In 1653, seven councilmen approved by Stuyvesant, two mayors, and a group of judges began to meet once a week. The local government listened to colonists' complaints and settled conflicts.

Dutch colonists built a wall at one end of Manhattan Island. The wall was later torn down and became Wall Street.

The colonists worked together to improve the city. They paved more roads, built new houses with tile roofs, and cleaned the streets. They built the colony's first hospital. Teachers, clothing merchants, and a doctor arrived with many other new colonists. Stuyvesant and the West India Company still ran the colony, but the colonists had a say in its future.

THE SURRENDER OF NEW AMSTERDAM

Stuyvesant worried about the safety of the colony. English colonists had moved into New Netherland territory. They were building towns in Connecticut and on Long Island. Stuyvesant wrote to the West India Company asking for more soldiers and gunpowder to defend New Amsterdam if they were attacked. The company did not have more soldiers to send.

In March 1664, King Charles II of England gave a North American land charter to his brother James, the Duke of York. The land included the colony of New Netherland. The English had plans to settle all of North America, and the port of New Amsterdam was important. British ships paid thousands of pounds to the West India Company to use the port.

James asked Colonel Richard Nicholls to take four gunboats and 450 soldiers to capture New Amsterdam.

The Hudson River emptied into the ocean at the port of New Amsterdam.

The operation moved quickly. By August, Nicholls had his ships blocking both the New Amsterdam port and the entrance to the Hudson River. He sent a letter to Stuyvesant demanding that he surrender all towns, forts, and lands of New Netherland to the king of England.

Stuyvesant had 16 cannons at the fort, but he was low on gunpowder. Messengers told him that armed English colonists had gathered in nearby Brooklyn. If it came to a battle, the Dutch were badly outnumbered. Stuyvesant met with the town council and a minister and talked with them about what to do. He was a soldier, and soldiers did not give up without a fight.

The colonists knew that many people would die and the town would be destroyed if Stuyvesant did not surrender. They cared more about their town and its people than the West India Company and Stuyvesant. Ninety-three

Dutch colonists pleaded with Stuyvesant not to fight the English.

town leaders sent a petition to Stuyvesant asking him to surrender. The names on the petition included Stuyvesant's son. The director-general said he "would much rather be carried out dead" than surrender.

In the end, Stuyvesant was the only person who wanted to fight the English. He agreed to surrender New Netherland. Nicholls brought his men ashore and raised the English flag over the fort. He proclaimed that the colony and city belonged to James, the Duke of York. Its new name would be New York.

The English changed little in the Dutch colony.

James, Duke of York

Dutch soldiers left New Amsterdam after surrendering it to the English.

The English recognized that New York was different from their other colonies. Many different nationalities, with different religions and languages, had somehow lived and worked together for 50 years. The Dutch valued tolerance, and that tolerance of differences helped build New Netherland into the thriving colony of New York.

GLOSSARY

alliance—agreement between nations or people to work together

charter—government grant that gives a monopoly on trade and profits to a particular individual or group of individuals for a particular place

diverse—differing by culture, religion, or race

monopoly—the right, granted by a court, to conduct business without competition

Northwest Passage—mythical sea route to Asia through the continent of North America

pelts—animal skins with the fur still on them

tolerant—open-minded

treaty—formal agreement between groups or nations

wampum—polished seashells used as money in the northeastern American colonies

DID YOU KNOW?

- One year after Henry Hudson explored New Netherland, he sailed to northern Canada in his search for the Northwest Passage. Despite the Arctic cold and thick ice, Hudson refused to turn back. His men rebelled and left Hudson, his young son, and a few others in a small boat with few supplies. Hudson and his group were never seen again.

- Many histories claim that Manhattan Island was purchased for 60 guilders, or around $24. No deed has been found for the sale of the island, though one letter mentions 60 guilders as the value of the trade goods that Peter Minuit gave the Lenape. Money was worth nothing to the Indians.

- During the 1600s, the Dutch owned a huge fleet of fishing and trade ships. From 1600 to 1750, the Netherlands had more ships than any other European country.

- In 1638, the king of Sweden hired Peter Minuit to start a colony on the Delaware River. Minuit bought some land along the Delaware River from the local Indians and built a fort, which he named after the Swedish princess, Christina. By 1655, New Sweden had grown to about 300 colonists when Peter Stuyvesant forced them to surrender to him. He reclaimed it for New Netherland.

IMPORTANT DATES

Timeline

1609	Henry Hudson explores the Delaware River, New York Bay, and the Hudson River and claims the land for the Netherlands.
1614	Dutch fur traders build Fort Nassau at the north end of the Hudson River.
1624	The Dutch West India Company sends the first colonists to New Netherland.
1626	Commander Peter Minuit moves the colony to Manhattan Island.
1638	William Kieft is named as the director-general of New Netherland.
1643–1645	Kieft's war with the Indians rages.
1647	Peter Stuyvesant is named director-general of New Netherland.
1653	The government in the Netherlands allows New Netherland colonists to form a local government.
1664	The English force Stuyvesant to surrender the colony of New Netherland; the English name it New York.

44

IMPORTANT PEOPLE

WILLIAM KIEFT (1597–1647)

Director-general of New Netherland from 1638 to 1647; he formed the Council of Twelve Men, the first representative body in New Netherland, to advise him on relations with Native Americans; he ignored the council's advice and started a war in 1643 that killed hundreds of Indians and colonists; Kieft died in a shipwreck off the coast of England

PETER MINUIT (1580–1638)

Director-general of New Netherland from 1626 to 1632; he purchased Manhattan Island from the Lenape Indians; born in present-day Germany, he moved to the Netherlands as a young man; he drowned at sea during a hurricane shortly after founding New Sweden

PETER STUYVESANT (1610?–1672)

Director-general of New Netherland from 1647 to 1664; raised and educated in the Netherlands, he joined the military and went to work for the Dutch West India Company; after surrending New Netherland to the English in 1664, he went to the Netherlands but later returned to New York and settled on his bouwerij *(farm); part of his farm later became the district of New York City called the Bowery*

WANT TO KNOW MORE?

More Books to Read

Doak, Robin S. *Hudson: Henry Hudson Searches for a Passage to Asia.*
Minneapolis: Compass Point Books, 2003.

Gibson, Karen Bush. *New Netherland: The Dutch Settle the Hudson Valley.*
Hockessin, Del.: Mitchell Lane Publishers, 2006.

Krizner, L.J., and Lisa Sita. *Peter Stuyvesant: New Amsterdam and the Origins
of New York.* New York: PowerKids Press, 2001.

McNeese, Tim. *New Amsterdam.* Philadelphia: Chelsea House
Publishers, 2007.

Parker, Lewis K. *Dutch Colonies in the Americas.* New York: PowerKids
Press, 2003.

On the Web

For more information on this topic, use FactHound.

1. Go to *www.facthound.com*

2. Type in this book ID: 0756538378

3. Click on the *Fetch It* button.

FactHound will find the best Web sites for you.

On the Road

Crailo State Historic Site

9½ Riverside Ave.
Rensselaer, NY 12144
518/463-8738
Artifacts from the Fort Orange archeological site near Albany, New York; guided tours and exhibits tell the story of early Dutch settlers

New York Unearthed

South Street Seaport Museum
17 State St.
New York, NY 10038
212/748-8757
Dioramas and artifacts representing 6,000 years of New York City history

Look for more We the People books about this era:

African-Americans in the Colonies

The California Missions

English Colonies in America

The French and Indian War

French Colonies in America

The Jamestown Colony

The Mayflower Compact

The Plymouth Colony

The Salem Witch Trials

Spanish Colonies in America

The Stamp Act of 1765

The Thirteen Colonies

Williamsburg

Women of Colonial America

A complete list of We the People titles is available on our Web site:
www.compasspointbooks.com

INDEX

About the Author

Mary Englar is a freelance writer and a teacher of English and creative writing. She has a master of fine arts degree in writing from Minnesota State University, and has written more than 30 nonfiction books for children. She lives in Minnesota, where she continues to read and write about the many different cultures of our world.